REAL ESTATE Exam PREP

2nd Edition

MISSOURI

While a great deal of care has been taken to provide accurate and current information, the ideas, suggestions, general principles, and conclusions presented in this text are subject to local, state and federal laws and regulations, court cases, and any revisions of same. The reader is urged to consult legal counsel regarding any points of law. This publication should not be used as a substitute for competent legal advice.

Publisher: Evan M. Butterfield
Senior Development Editor: Kristen Short
Development Editor: Amanda Rahn
Development Editor: David Cirillo
Associate Development Editor: Michael J. Scafuri
Production Manager: Bryan Samolinski
Creative Director: Lucy Jenkins
Cover Design: Gail Chandler

Testbank Reviewer: Randy Bateman
Question Consultant: Bruce H. Aydt, ABR, ABRM, CRB
Exam Prep Series Content Consultant: Marie Spodek, DREI

Copyright 2002 by Dearborn Financial Publishing, Inc.®

Published by Dearborn™ Real Estate Education
a division of Dearborn Financial Publishing, Inc.®
155 North Wacker Drive
Chicago, IL 60606-1719
http://www.dearbornRE.com

All rights reserved. The text of this publication, or any part thereof, may not be reproduced in any manner whatsoever without written permission from the publisher.

Printed in the United States of America.

02 03 04   10 9 8 7 6 5 4 3 2 1

Introduction

Welcome to *Missouri Exam Prep*! When you bought this book, you showed that you are serious about passing the exam and getting your real estate license. This is *NOT* an easy test. For people whose test-taking skills are weak, or who haven't adequately prepared, the exam can be a nightmare. For those who have taken the time and effort to study and review, however, the exam can be a much more positive experience.

It's pretty obvious, though, that if you practice and review key material, your test score will improve. This book is your key to exam success.

The process is simple: Just work your way through the practice questions, taking your time and answering each one carefully. Then check your answers by studying the Answer Key, where you'll find both the correct answer to each question as well as an explanation of *why* that answer is correct. It might be a good idea to review your classroom materials and textbook before you start.

Remember: These 200 questions reflect as closely as possible the topic coverage of the state-specific portion of your exam only! For the balance of the test, you'll need to use a "national" exam prep book. And remember, too, that it takes study and hard work on your part to pass the licensing exam: no single study aid will do the trick alone.

Experts who are familiar with the Missouri licensing examination, as well as real estate law and practice, prepared this book. You've taken the first step toward your success as a real estate professional: Good Luck!

Dearborn Real Estate Education

Missouri *Exam Prep*

1. Mark, a licensed broker, procures a ready, willing, and able buyer for his seller-principal. The seller accepts the buyer's offer in writing, then experiences a change of heart and refuses to close. In this situation, Mark

   A. may sue to collect the commission from the seller.
   B. is without recourse because the transaction was never completed.
   C. may sue the buyer.
   D. may retain the deposit as commission.

2. A real estate company has entered into agency agreements with both a seller and a buyer. The buyer is interested in making an offer on the seller's property. Can this occur?

   A. No, because the real estate company would then be a dual agent
   B. Yes, as long as written agency agreements have been entered into with both parties
   C. Yes, if the seller has agreed to pay the commission
   D. Yes, if the buyer and seller both give their consent to dual agency

3. In a cobroker transaction, the selling broker is a subagent of the listing broker and, as such, works for the seller. When must the selling broker make written disclosure of this fact to the buyer?

   A. Before showing property to the buyer
   B. Before closing the transaction
   C. No later than when the buyer signs an offer to purchase a property
   D. When first providing assistance or taking information from the buyer

4. A buyer wants to purchase a home from a seller but has not yet entered into a contractual agreement to do so. The buyer and seller ask a real estate broker to assist them in the transaction, including working out the terms of the contract and closing the transaction. May the broker close the transaction and be paid a commission for these activities?

   A. Yes, because a broker is permitted to close real estate transactions
   B. Yes, because the broker can assist the buyer and seller as a transaction broker
   C. No, because a broker is not permitted to close real estate transactions
   D. No, because the broker is not an agent for either the buyer or seller and did not negotiate the transaction

5. A broker represented a seller under an exclusive-right-to-sell listing agreement. This broker made an oral agreement with another broker, who represented a buyer, to split the commission should the second broker find a suitable buyer. One month later the second broker found a suitable buyer for the property. Which of the following is true?

   A. The first broker represents the seller and the second broker represents the buyer.
   B. The second broker represents the seller and the first broker represents the buyer.
   C. Both brokers represent the buyer.
   D. Both brokers represent the seller.

6. A transaction broker represents which of the following?

   A. Buyer
   B. Seller
   C. Neither the buyer nor the seller
   D. Both the buyer and the seller

7. A transaction broker is responsible for which of the following?

   A. Advising the buyer
   B. Advising the seller
   C. Presenting all offers in a timely manner
   D. Providing the buyer's motivating factors to the seller

8. A seller signs a listing agreement that does not provide for representation. This is an example of

   A. dual agency.
   B. special agency.
   C. transaction brokerage.
   D. seller's limited agency.

9. A seller's listing agreement has expired, and the seller lists with a different brokerage firm. Jim, the original listing agent, now has a buyer interested in the seller's property. Based on this information, Jim

   A. is a dual agent.
   B. cannot disclose to the buyer offers received on the seller's property while it was listed with him.
   C. cannot disclose to the buyer information about the physical condition of the property.
   D. cannot represent the buyer.

10. A real estate salesperson has been working with buyers. After helping them negotiate for their dream home, the buyers ask the salesperson if she can help them secure a mortgage. The salesperson knows a lender that pays a fee for referring purchasers to it. Can the salesperson accept the fee for referring the buyers to this lender?

    A. No, because a referral fee or kickback is prohibited by the Real Estate Settlement Procedures Act (RESPA), and a salesperson can accept compensation only from his or her broker
    B. Yes, if the salesperson and the buyers have previously entered into a written buyer agency agreement
    C. Yes, if the salesperson discloses the referral fee to the sellers
    D. Yes, if the lender offers the market's best interest rates and terms

11. A buyer prospect is interested in seeing a house listed with the real estate company, but does not wish to enter into a buyer agency agreement. A salesperson from the real estate company can show the buyer an in-house listing if the

    A. salesperson obtains the seller's permission.
    B. buyer verbally agrees to buyer agency.
    C. salesperson provides the buyer with an agency disclosure that the real estate company represents the seller.
    D. salesperson provides the buyer with a dual agency consent form.

12. In Missouri, an exclusive-right-to-buy contract

    A. is illegal.
    B. is equivalent to a listing agreement.
    C. must be indicated as such in the buyer agency agreement.
    D. requires the signature of the principal only.

13. Buyer's limited agent contracts in Missouri

    A. must be in writing to be in compliance with the license law's agency provisions.
    B. must be on forms approved by the Missouri Real Estate Commission.
    C. are not regulated under the license laws.
    D. are illegal.

14. All of the following provisions are included in the Missouri Real Estate Commission's rules regarding listing agreements EXCEPT that

    A. a listing agreement must state the exact fee the broker will earn.
    B. a listing agreement must be accompanied by a qualified expert's report of the property's condition.
    C. a listing agreement must be in writing and signed by both broker and seller.
    D. the seller must receive a true copy of the listing agreement after signing it.

15. In a dual agency situation, a broker may collect a commission from both the seller and the buyer if

    A. the broker holds a state license.
    B. the buyer and the seller are related by blood or marriage.
    C. both parties give their signed, contractual consent to the dual compensation.
    D. both parties are represented by attorneys.

16. A buyer, working with a salesperson from LMN Realty, is interested in seeing a house listed with XYZ Realty but does not wish to enter into an agency relationship with LMN. The salesperson can show the buyer the house if

    A. XYZ Realty obtains the seller's written consent to cooperate with transaction brokers or subagents, the buyer is given a Missouri Brokerage Disclosure Form, and the salesperson discloses the brokerage relationship (transaction broker or subagent) that LMN will be using.
    B. XYZ Realty and LMN Realty do not have a subagency agreement, and the buyer is given a Missouri Brokerage Disclosure Form stating that XYZ Realty represents the seller.
    C. the buyer verbally agrees to buyer agency.
    D. This cannot occur.

17. Seller property condition disclosures should be delivered to the buyer

    A. prior to the buyer's making a written offer.
    B. at the time that the seller agrees to the offer.
    C. at the time of the home inspection.
    D. prior to closing.

18. A licensed salesperson is at a party. During idle conversation, another person at the party states she wants to buy a home. The salesperson offers to sell her his home. For him to sell her his home, he would be required to

   A. inform his broker.
   B. disclose to her that he is a licensed salesperson.
   C. charge her no commission because it is his home.
   D. sell the property at the full market value.

19. When listing property, a broker noticed a crack in a basement wall that was covered by boxes. When showing the property to potential buyers, the licensee must

   A. inform the prospective buyers of the crack.
   B. inform the prospective buyers of the crack only if they ask.
   C. not inform prospective buyers of the crack because the licensee represents the seller.
   D. move the boxes so that the crack is not hidden and can be discovered by the buyers.

20. A salesperson arranges for his fiancee to purchase property at the full listed price. The salesperson does not disclose to the seller the fact that he is engaged to the buyer. Did the salesperson violate the law?

   A. Yes, because a salesperson must disclose any ownership interest that he or she will have (i.e., after the marriage) and must disclose his or her status as a licensee.
   B. Yes, because an agent may not buy property for his fiancee
   C. No, because he does not have to reveal his marital intentions
   D. No, because he is only required to disclose his status as a licensee

21. A salesperson with an inactive license wants to buy property. The salesperson contacts an out-of-state broker and makes an offer on property located out of state. Who must be advised of the salesperson's status as a licensee?

   A. Listing broker
   B. Seller
   C. Selling broker
   D. No one because the salesperson is inactive

22. A buyer may reasonably rely on which of the following facts communicated by a salesperson concerning commercial property?

   A. Only those communicated in writing by mail
   B. Only past and present income generated by the property
   C. Unseen structural defects, but not obvious defects
   D. Any adverse material fact of which the licensee has knowledge or, if a buyer's agent, or which the agent should have known

23. A salesperson represents a seller in a transaction. When prospective buyers ask to look at the property, the salesperson must

    A. tell them that they must first enter into a buyer representation agreement with another licensee.
    B. inform them in writing that the salesperson represents the seller's interests.
    C. inform them orally that the salesperson represents the seller's interests.
    D. show them the property without making any disclosures about the salesperson's relationship with the seller, because such disclosure would be a violation of the salesperson's fiduciary duties.

24. A broker took a listing for a small office building. Because the property is in excellent condition and produces a good, steady income, the broker's salesperson has decided to purchase it as an investment. If the broker's salesperson wishes to buy this property, the salesperson must

    A. resign as the broker's agent and make an offer after the owner has retained another broker.
    B. have some third party purchase the property on the salesperson's behalf so that the owner does not learn the true identity of the purchaser.
    C. obtain permission from the Missouri Real Estate Commission.
    D. inform the owner in writing that the salesperson is a licensee.

25. Six months after a buyer bought a house, the roof leaked during a rainstorm. When the house was listed, the seller told the broker that the roof leaked, but they agreed not to tell any prospective buyers. The broker claims that the buyer did not ask about the roof. Under these facts, the buyer

    A. can sue the broker and file a complaint against the broker with the real estate commission for the failure to disclose.
    B. cannot sue the broker or file a complaint with the real estate commission against the broker.
    C. can sue the seller under license law.
    D. cannot do anything because the leaking roof could have been discovered by inspection.

26. A real estate licensee must give the Missouri Broker Disclosure Form to prospective purchasers/tenants

    A. upon obtaining personal or financial information, or before the signing of a brokerage service agreement, whichever comes first.
    B. at an open house.
    C. at the closing table.
    D. before any offers to purchase or lease are prepared or presented.

27. A real estate licensee has signed a brokerage agreement with a tenant who is looking for an apartment to rent. The licensee does not charge a fee to prospective tenants; rather, the licensee receives a commission from landlords. The licensee tells a landlord that the prospective tenant could probably pay a somewhat higher rent than the landlord is asking. Which of the following statements is true?

    A. The licensee owes the fiduciary agency duties to the landlords who pay the commission.
    B. The licensee's disclosure to the landlord was appropriate under these circumstances.
    C. The licensee's disclosure violated the fiduciary duties owed to the tenant.
    D. Because the licensee is not charging a fee to prospective tenants, the licensee has violated Missouri agency statute.

28. A licensed salesperson obtains a listing. Several days later, the salesperson meets prospective buyers at the property and tells them, "I am the listing agent for this property and so I represent the seller. Because I'm the listing agent, I'm very familiar with the property." Under these circumstances, the salesperson

    A. has failed to properly disclose his or her agency relationship.
    B. has properly disclosed his or her agency relationship with the seller.
    C. is in violation of Missouri regulations, because the listing belongs to the broker.
    D. has created a dual agency, which is a violation of Missouri regulations.

29. A realty company has entered into agency agreements with both a seller and a buyer. The seller and the buyer have signed the dual agency consent agreement. The salesperson with the realty company has been working with the buyer. The salesperson may

    A. provide comparable market data to the seller and buyer.
    B. disclose the buyer's financial qualifications to the seller.
    C. disclose to the buyer that the seller will accept less than the listing price.
    D. disclose to the seller that the buyer will pay more than the offering price.

30. A brokerage's relationship with a seller as an agent must be determined and all necessary agreements executed

    A. at any time after a purchase and sale agreement is executed by the parties.
    B. before engaging in any brokerage activities for that seller.
    C. no later than the time a purchase and sale agreement is prepared.
    D. no later than the closing.

31. A buyer, who is a client of a broker, wants to purchase a house that the broker has listed for sale. Which of the following statements is true?

    A. If the listing salesperson and selling salesperson are two different people, there is no problem.
    B. The broker should refer the buyer to another broker to negotiate the sale.
    C. The seller and buyer must be informed of the situation and agree to the broker's representing both of them.
    D. The buyer should not have been shown a house listed by the broker.

32. In Missouri, all of the following would be grounds for revoking a broker's license EXCEPT

    A. being convicted of a felony.
    B. advertising in a newspaper that he or she is a member of the Missouri Association of Real Estate Professionals when in fact he or she is not.
    C. depositing escrow money into his or her personal checking account.
    D. agreeing with a seller to accept a listing for more than the broker's published commission rate.

33. The commission has the power to revoke a salesperson's license if the salesperson

    A. enters into a dual agency agreement.
    B. attempts to represent a buyer.
    C. enters into an exclusive-listing contract.
    D. deposits a buyer's down payment into his or her own bank account.

34. In Missouri, a broker may have his or her license suspended or revoked for all of the following actions EXCEPT

    A. being declared mentally incompetent.
    B. depositing earnest money into the firm's escrow account.
    C. helping another person cheat on the licensing examination.
    D. displaying a "For Sale" sign on a property without the owner's consent.

35. A person has been convicted of embezzlement. Which of the following is true?

    A. The Missouri Real Estate Commission may refuse to grant that person a license.
    B. The person may not attend a prelicense school.
    C. The person may not take the prelicense examination.
    D. The person may apply for a salesperson's license but not a broker's license.

36. A motel clerk provides a broker friend the names of guests staying at the motel who are going to be moving into the area and are looking for homes to buy. The broker pays the clerk a small fee for the referrals. Is paying a referral fee legal?

    A. No, because the motel clerk would be violating his fiduciary duty to the motel owner
    B. No, because it is illegal for a broker to pay a referral fee
    C. Yes, if the motel clerk is licensed with the broker
    D. Yes, if the owner of the motel gives his consent

37. A salesperson licensed in another state but not licensed in Missouri comes into Missouri and sells property located in Missouri. She is entitled to

    A. a full commission because she is licensed.
    B. half the commission because her broker would be entitled to the other half.
    C. a commission based on her agreement with her broker.
    D. no commission because she is not licensed in Missouri.

38. A broker sold a home to first-time buyers and helped them apply for a "bond" money loan. Because the buyers were $2,000 short of having sufficient cash for the down payment, the broker decided to write two contracts: one for the lender that included $2,000 of the down payment in the loan and the other for the actual sales price that did not include the $2,000. This is

    A. allowable because all parties would be involved in both contracts.
    B. allowable as long as it was in the form of a contract.
    C. a violation of Missouri law, and the Missouri Real Estate Commission could revoke the broker's license.
    D. a violation of Missouri law for a first-time homebuyer to finance the purchase with bond money.

39. A newly licensed salesperson obtained permission from friends and relatives to place a "For Sale" sign in their yards. When potential buyers inquire about a property, the salesperson told them the property was sold but she would be happy to help them find another property suitable for their wants and needs. Is this permissible?

    A. Yes, because this is simply a clever sales technique
    B. Yes, as long as she has the friends' and relatives' written permission
    C. No, because the properties were not sold
    D. No, since the properties were not actually for sale, this constitutes false advertising.

40. The Missouri Real Estate Commission has received a sworn written complaint against a broker on the proper complaint form. The Missouri Real Estate Commission may do all of the following EXCEPT

    A. subpoena the broker.
    B. subpoena the broker's business accounts and records.
    C. pay expenses and fees to witnesses who attend a Missouri Real Estate Commission investigatory hearing.
    D. suspend the broker's license.

41. If a licensee violates any portion of Chapter 339, all of the following are possible EXCEPT that the

    A. violation is a Class B misdemeanor.
    B. violator may be subject to fine under the jurisdiction of a proper court.
    C. violator may be subject to civil liability to the aggrieved person.
    D. violator may be confined to prison by action of the Missouri Real Estate Commission.

42. Which of the following happens after a licensee has been found guilty of violating the license law?

    A. The Missouri Real Estate Commission may publish a summary report of the administrative hearing commission decision.
    B. The administrative hearing commission may set the penalties assessed against the licensee.
    C. Information gained in the investigations of the licensee may be made available to the general public.
    D. The Missouri Real Estate Commission may not make public the decisions of the administrative hearing commission.

43. An unlicensed person is selling real estate for another and for compensation in Missouri. She is guilty of which of the following?

    A. Felony
    B. Misdemeanor
    C. Either a felony or misdemeanor
    D. Neither a felony nor misdemeanor

44. If a broker tells a lender that the sales price on a property is something above its actual sales price, the

    A. broker has done nothing wrong as long as the appraisal substantiates this price.
    B. buyer is likely to receive an interest rate break.
    C. broker can lose his or her license and be fined.
    D. buyer can receive a higher mortgage amount.

45. A salesperson listed a property and put a sign in the yard with his name and phone number. The sign must also contain which of the following?

    A. Broker's name and telephone number
    B. Broker's name
    C. Broker's telephone number
    D. Broker's name, address, and telephone number

46. A broker places the following TV advertisement: "List your home with Ajax Realty and if we don't sell your home, we'll buy it from you." This may lead to revocation of the broker's license because

    A. the commercial was not approved by the Missouri Real Estate Commission.
    B. it is illegal for a broker to buy properties listed with the broker.
    C. there was not sufficient information in the advertisement to comply with the Missouri Real Estate Commission rules and regulations.
    D. the Missouri Real Estate Commission does not permit the advertisement of guaranteed sales plans.

47. A salesperson is selling his home by himself without listing it with a broker. The salesperson is licensed with Ford Realty. The salesperson wants to put a sign in his yard. Which of the following must appear on the sign?

    A. "For Sale by Owner, 555-6666"
    B. "For Sale by Owner, call Realty Co., 555-5555"
    C. "For Sale by Owner"
    D. "For Sale by Owner/Salesperson"

48. A person owns Ajax Realty and is advertising property. Which advertisement is acceptable?

    A. "For Sale, call Ajax Realty, 555-2222"
    B. "For Sale, call 555-2222"
    C. "For Sale by Owner, call 555-2222"
    D. "For Sale by Owner"

49. A broker who wishes to place a "For Sale" sign on a listed property must first

    A. obtain the property owner's consent.
    B. sell the property.
    C. list the property.
    D. get the neighbors' permission.

50. Listings based on a "net price" are
    A. more profitable because no minimum is set on the amount of commission collectible.
    B. legal in Missouri as long as the seller agrees.
    C. illegal in Missouri at any time.
    D. permissible with approval of the commission.

51. A seller told a broker that she wanted to clear $50,000 when she sold her house. The broker accepted the listing and sold it for $160,000. He gave $50,000 to the seller and kept the rest. Which of the following is correct?
    A. The broker should have given the seller a better appraisal of the value of her house.
    B. The broker's commission exceeds statutory and NAR guidelines.
    C. The broker accepted an illegal net listing.
    D. As the seller's agent, the broker had a duty to sell the house for as much as possible.

52. Two brokers have a dispute over how to split the commission. One of the brokers filed a complaint with the Missouri Real Estate Commission. The Missouri Real Estate Commission
    A. may revoke the license of the listing broker, who withheld the commission.
    B. will settle the dispute at its next meeting.
    C. will not enter into the dispute.
    D. will make a recommendation as to how to split the commission but will not make a ruling.

53. Two brokers have a dispute as to which broker is entitled to a commission in a real estate transaction. Both brokers filed an appeal with the Missouri Real Estate Commission to settle the dispute. Which of the following would the Missouri Real Estate Commission most likely do?
    A. It will report the dispute to the administrative hearing commission, which will then recommend what action the Missouri Real Estate Commission should take.
    B. It will report the dispute to the attorney general, who will instruct the Missouri Real Estate Commission as to what action to take.
    C. The Missouri Real Estate Commission will not become involved in disputes between licensees concerning commissions.
    D. The Missouri Real Estate Commission will negotiate the dispute when requested by the brokers.

54. A subagent sells a home in a cooperative transaction. Which of the following is true of the commission?
    A. The commission is paid directly to the subagent.
    B. The subagent is not due a commission because he is a subagent.
    C. The commission is paid to the listing broker.
    D. The commission is split between the buyer and seller.

55. A broker may pay compensation for negotiating the sale of property to a(n)
    A. attorney.
    B. friend.
    C. salesperson licensed under the broker.
    D. salesperson licensed under another broker.

56. In Missouri, real estate commissions are
    A. set by law.
    B. set by the Missouri Real Estate Commission.
    C. determined by local groups of brokers.
    D. negotiable between the seller and buyer and broker.

57. Commissions earned by a broker in a real estate sales transaction
    A. are determined by agreement of the broker and his or her principal.
    B. may be shared with an unlicensed person, provided that such person aided the broker in bringing the buyer and seller together.
    C. may be deducted from the earnest money deposit and claimed by the broker as soon as the buyer and seller execute the purchase and sales agreement.
    D. are based on a schedule of commission rates set by the Missouri Real Estate Commission.

58. A salesperson secures an offer on property listed with her broker. The salesperson should have the earnest money check made payable to the
    A. listing broker and held by the salesperson until there is an agreement between the parties.
    B. broker or other entity specified in the offer. If the listing broker is specified, the licensee should transmit the earnest money to the broker immediately.
    C. listing broker and deposited into the salesperson's escrow account.
    D. salesperson and signed over to the broker immediately.

59. A broker received earnest money on a real estate transaction for a friend. If the broker deposited the money into his personal account, this would be
    A. misrepresentation.
    B. commingling.
    C. waste.
    D. a felony.

60. A salesperson must deliver earnest money to his or her broker
    A. immediately.
    B. within two banking days.
    C. within five banking days.
    D. within seven banking days.

61. In the event of a dispute over earnest money, the broker should
    A. release the money to the person stated in the contract.
    B. release the money to the seller according to the broker's fiduciary responsibility.
    C. hold the money until both parties sign a release.
    D. hold the money until all parties to the contract sign a release.

62. A broker's escrow account must be located in
    A. a bank in the state of Missouri.
    B. a bank in the state of Missouri if it is an interest-bearing account.
    C. a bank in the state of Missouri or, with the Missouri Real Estate Commission's permission, in a bank in an adjoining state.
    D. any state approved by the Missouri Real Estate Commission.

63. Eight days after a buyer and seller reach an agreement, the buyer asks the broker to hold the earnest money for five additional days. This
   A. is against the law.
   B. requires 15 percent down.
   C. requires seller approval.
   D. may be for only three days.

64. A licensed broker acting as a property manager must deposit current rent money into a(n)
   A. escrow account.
   B. business account.
   C. property management escrow account.
   D. operating account.

65. A licensed broker, managing property for the owner, receives an allowance from the owner for maintenance. The money would be deposited into the
   A. escrow account.
   B. repair account.
   C. operating account.
   D. property management escrow account.

66. All funds received by a broker on behalf of his or her principal must be deposited into an escrow or trust account within
   A. three days of receiving the offer.
   B. three days of obtaining all signatures on the contract.
   C. five working days of receiving the offer.
   D. ten banking days of receiving all signatures.

67. A broker manages three properties for the same owner. One property is in need of emergency repairs, but there is not enough money in the management account to cover the cost. The broker borrows money from the escrow account of one of the other properties to make the repairs. Which of the following is true?
   A. The broker has acted properly by safeguarding the client's interest.
   B. Such action is proper when the same person owns all properties.
   C. The broker is in violation of regulations for handling escrow funds improperly.
   D. The broker must use personal funds for repairs if there is not enough money in the management account.

68. In Missouri, brokers and salespeople who are not lawyers may
   A. complete a bill of sale after a sales contract has been signed.
   B. fill in blanks on preprinted form contracts approved by the broker's counsel.
   C. suggest additional language to be added to a preprinted sales contract by a buyer or seller.
   D. explain the legal significance of specific preprinted contract clauses to a buyer or seller.

69. Standardized forms used in a real estate transaction may be prepared or approved by
   A. the Board of REALTORS®.
   B. the broker's attorney.
   C. the real estate commission.
   D. any attorney.

70. A broker takes a listing from a seller. The broker must give the seller a copy of the listing agreement

    A. at the time of signing.
    B. the next business day.
    C. within three business days.
    D. at the time an offer is presented.

71. All of the following are required of listing agreements in Missouri EXCEPT that

    A. listing agreements may not have automatic extensions.
    B. listing agreements must have a specific expiration date.
    C. a copy of the listing agreement must be given to the seller at the time of signing.
    D. both the buyer and seller must sign the listing agreement.

72. All of the following must appear in a written listing agreement EXCEPT the

    A. commission to be paid the broker.
    B. complete legal description of the property being sold.
    C. time duration of the listing.
    D. price.

73. A broker signs a listing agreement with a seller. The agreement contains the following clause: "If the Property has not been sold after three months from the date of this signing, this agreement will automatically continue for additional three-month periods thereafter until the property is sold." Based on these facts, the agreement

    A. is legal under Missouri law, because it contains a reference to a specific time limit.
    B. is illegal in Missouri.
    C. automatically receives a statutory six-month listing period for this open listing in Missouri.
    D. is legal under Missouri law, because the list periods are for less than six months each.

74. Regarding listing agreements in Missouri, which of the following could result in the suspension or revocation of a licensee's license to practice real estate?

    A. A specified commission rate
    B. No specific termination date
    C. No broker protection clause
    D. A specific termination date

75. Upon obtaining a listing, a broker or licensed salesperson is obligated to

    A. set up a listing file and issue it a number in compliance with Missouri Real Estate license law and rules.
    B. place advertisements in the local newspapers.
    C. cooperate with every real estate office wishing to participate in the marketing of the listed property.
    D. give the seller signing the listing a legible, signed, true, and correct copy.

76. A seller listed his house for sale with a broker on February 1. The listing agreement was to last five months. In April, the seller decided that the house was no longer for sale. Which of the following statements is true?

    A. The seller has canceled the agreement and there are no penalties.
    B. The seller has withdrawn the broker's authority to sell the property and may be subject to a payment for time and expenses.
    C. The seller is required by law to leave his house on the market until June.
    D. The Missouri Real Estate Commission will decide if the seller's action is justifiable.

77. A broker closed his real estate business because he went to work for another broker as a broker-salesperson. Now he wants to go back into business for himself. What must he do?

    A. Send a transfer form to the Missouri Real Estate Commission for transfer to a broker-individual license
    B. Send his license to the Missouri Real Estate Commission for transfer to inactive broker-salesperson status
    C. Pass the broker examination to transfer to a broker-individual license
    D. Attend a broker prelicense school and pass the broker examination to transfer to broker-individual

78. A salesperson working for a broker may

    A. auction real estate directly for an owner.
    B. accept compensation directly from another broker.
    C. accept compensation directly from an owner of listed property.
    D. pay compensation to another salesperson who assisted in the sale of property.

79. A salesperson is a subagent of a broker in a transaction. Is the salesperson entitled to a commission if he or she sells the house?

    A. No, if there is no written agreement with the listing broker
    B. No, if there is no written agreement with the seller
    C. Yes, from his or her own broker
    D. Yes, from the seller

80. Assuming the salesperson is NOT working in a designated agency relationship, the salesperson may be an agent of

    A. another salesperson.
    B. his or her broker.
    C. a buyer.
    D. a seller.

81. A Missouri real estate salesperson may lawfully collect compensation from

    A. either a buyer or a seller.
    B. the employing broker only.
    C. any party to the transaction or the party's representative.
    D. a licensed real estate broker only.

82. A licensed salesperson may hold a concurrent license with more than one Missouri broker under which of the following circumstances?

    A. Under no circumstances
    B. With the permission of his or her sales manager
    C. With the written consent of the brokers being represented
    D. With the permission of the real estate commission

83. Several weeks after a closing, a broker-salesperson received a thank-you letter and a nice bonus check from the seller of the house. The broker-salesperson cashed the check because she felt it was earned. In this situation, which of the following is true?

    A. The broker-salesperson may accept the bonus because she is licensed as an associate broker.
    B. Accepting the money is allowed if more than 30 days have elapsed since the closing.
    C. The broker-salesperson may accept the money if her broker permits her to do so.
    D. Accepting the money is a violation of the license law.

84. When a sole proprietor has his or her license suspended for two years, what effect does this have on the broker-salespersons and salespeople affiliated with the proprietor?

    A. Affiliates' licenses will be revoked, subject to reinstatement after one year.
    B. Affiliates' licenses will also be suspended for a two-year period.
    C. Suspension has no effect on the affiliates.
    D. Affiliates' licenses must be returned to the real estate commission.

85. A broker opened a branch office. Of the following, who can manage the branch office?

    A. Broker-salesperson
    B. Salesperson
    C. Any person so designated by the owner
    D. Any licensee

86. The licenses of affiliated salespeople may be kept in all of the following places EXCEPT the

    A. reception area of the salesperson's office.
    B. unused salesperson's office next to the salesperson's office.
    C. boardroom of the salesperson's office.
    D. salesperson's possession, to be displayed on request.

87. For a change to be made, a broker must provide the Missouri Real Estate Commission with which of the following information concerning her branch offices?

    A. The name and address of the licensee in charge of each branch office
    B. The address of each branch office and the name of the licensee in charge of each branch office
    C. The name and address of the principal broker
    D. The name of each branch office if different from the principal broker and the name of the licensee in charge of each branch office

88. A broker was involved in so many lawsuits that he decided to change the name of his branch offices to avoid problems for those offices not involved in the lawsuits. May he do this?

    A. Yes, with the approval of the Missouri Real Estate Commission
    B. Yes, provided all advertising is done in both names
    C. No, because all branch offices must have the same name as the parent office
    D. No, because the Missouri Real Estate Commission assigns the name for each branch office

89. A broker intends to open a branch office in a neighboring town. The broker sends the real estate commission notice of the new branch office, giving a name that clearly identifies its relationship with his main office. The broker names a licensed real estate salesperson as the branch office manager. Under these facts, is the broker in compliance with the license law?

    A. Yes, the broker has fully complied with the requirements of the license law.
    B. No, under the license law, brokers cannot have branch offices in more than one municipality.
    C. Yes, by naming the salesperson as the branch's manager, the broker is in compliance with the requirement that a broker may be in direct operational control of only one office or branch.
    D. No, the manager of a branch office must be a licensed real estate broker.

90. A broker-salesperson is not satisfied with her present real estate company and has decided to become associated with another. Before the broker-salesperson can begin actively selling for the new company, the

    A. first broker must transfer the broker salesperson's license to the new office.
    B. new broker must notify the commission of the change and send in the proper forms and fees.
    C. broker-salesperson must take her license to the new brokerage and notify the commission, within three days, of the transfer to a new location.
    D. broker-salesperson's old license, along with the proper fee and form signed by the new broker, must be sent to the commission and the new license returned to the second broker.

91. When a licensed broker changes his or her place of business,

    A. a new license will be issued by the board immediately.
    B. his or her license may be revoked if the Missouri Real Estate Commission is not notified.
    C. a new license will be issued for a full term.
    D. the new address must be approved by the board.

92. A buyer and seller not under contract with any broker ask a broker to fill in a contract that reflects the terms of their agreement. The broker may

    A. not fill in the contract because he or she is not acting as the broker in the transaction, buy only as a document preparer.
    B. not fill in the contract for a fee.
    C. fill in the contract and charge his or her normal fee.
    D. fill in the contract if he or she does not charge a fee.

93. In any real estate sales transaction that a broker negotiates, the broker is not required to

    A. inform the buyer of his or her personal opinion of the condition of the seller's title to the property.
    B. make sure that the written purchase agreement includes all the terms of the parties' agreement.
    C. make sure that the closing statement is accurate and that a copy of it is delivered to both buyer and seller.
    D. keep copies of all documents involved in the transaction in his or her files for three years after the year in which the transaction was closed.

94. In the typical listing arrangement, which of the following are required for a broker to be entitled to a commission in a civil court action?

    A. A signed listing agreement
    B. A ready, willing, and able buyer
    C. A closing of title by the purchaser
    D. A binding contract between the seller and purchaser

95. Every Missouri real estate office is required to

    A. maintain escrow account records for five years.
    B. keep transaction records for three years.
    C. employ at least one salesperson.
    D. There are no requirements for real estate offices in Missouri.

96. A real estate company refers all of its title insurance business to a title company. Each month the title company pays a small fee to the real estate company for the referrals. This is

    A. a kickback, but it is not excessive so it is not illegal.
    B. an illegal kickback under federal law.
    C. permitted because the fee is small.
    D. permitted because it is a friendly business practice to charge a small fee to pay the broker's expenses.

97. Under the terms of a sales contract, a seller is required to provide a termite certificate. The seller requests that the salesperson order one. The salesperson does so, knowing she will receive a referral fee from the pest control company. Is this a violation of the license law?

    A. No, if the fee is less than $25
    B. No, if the fee is disclosed, either orally or in writing, to the parties to the contract
    C. Yes, because a salesperson may not receive a referral fee from anyone other than her employing broker
    D. Yes, because special fees may be paid to the salesperson only by the seller

98. An airline pilot told a broker about some friends who were looking for a new home. The broker contacted the friends and eventually sold them a house. When may the broker pay the airline pilot for this valuable lead?

    A. As soon as a valid sales contract is signed by the parties
    B. Only after the sale closes
    C. After the funds are released from escrow
    D. The broker may not pay the airline pilot for the lead.

99. Which is true when two brokers cooperate on the sale of a property?

    A. There must be a written agreement between the brokers.
    B. The selling broker may be a subagent of the listing broker.
    C. The listing broker is a subagent of the selling broker.
    D. The selling broker is normally compensated directly by the seller.

100. A broker wants to transfer to inactive status to open a restaurant. She may
    A. maintain her real estate business.
    B. not maintain her real estate business.
    C. refer clients to another broker and receive a referral fee.
    D. not go inactive unless she is sponsored by another broker.

101. A new broker is considering opening his office in his home. With which of the following must the broker comply?
    A. The broker may employ only two salespersons.
    B. The office must be open to the public during regular business hours or at regularly stated intervals.
    C. A broker may not have his office in his home.
    D. An office in the broker's home must have a separate entrance.

102. After successfully negotiating an offer and a counteroffer, a salesperson returns to her office to make copies of the documents. The salesperson discovers that one of the parties did not sign the final document. The salesperson should
    A. go back and have the party sign the final document.
    B. not worry because all parties agreed to the terms of the final document.
    C. have the document signed at closing.
    D. sign the document for the party.

103. Which of the following statements is an example of puffing and would not be considered a license law violation?
    A. Told a buyer that a restaurant near the property was "the best in town"
    B. Did not tell a buyer of a pending rezoning of the property
    C. Told a seller not to tell the buyer of a leaking roof
    D. Deposited earnest money into one's personal account for safekeeping until there was an agreement between the buyer and seller

104. How is the broker's commission determined in a real estate sales transaction?
    A. It must be stated in the listing agreement and is negotiated between the broker and seller.
    B. It is determined according to the standard rates set by agreement of local real estate brokers.
    C. If under dispute, it will be determined through arbitration by the Missouri Real Estate Commission.
    D. It must be paid with cash or a cashier's check on closing.

105. All of the following agreements must be in writing EXCEPT a(n)
    A. exclusive-agency listing.
    B. open listing.
    C. exclusive-right-to-sell agreement.
    D. multiple listing.

106. In Missouri, the real estate license law is administered by the
    A. Council on Housing Matters.
    B. Missouri Real Estate Commission.
    C. Missouri Association of REALTORS®.
    D. Department of Housing and Urban Development (HUD).

107. How are members of the Missouri Real Estate Commission selected?

    A. By the governor
    B. By public election
    C. By the state association of REALTORS®
    D. Elected by real estate licensees

108. The real estate commission has the authority to

    A. make and enforce the rules by which all real estate licensees must abide.
    B. compose the examination questions on the state exam.
    C. administer the exams given at the testing sites.
    D. enact the laws that govern real estate licensees.

109. A seller who listed his property with the real estate office telephoned the Missouri Real Estate Commission to file a complaint against the real estate office. The Missouri Real Estate Commission sent him a complaint form to fill out, but he did not return the form. The Missouri Real Estate Commission could

    A. act or not act on the phone call at its own discretion.
    B. be prohibited from following up on an oral complaint.
    C. be required to ignore the oral complaint.
    D. be required to act on the oral complaint.

110. A complaint is filed against a real estate broker. The Missouri Real Estate Commission may do all of the following EXCEPT

    A. pay expenses and fees of witnesses who attend any investigatory hearings.
    B. subpoena the business records and accounts of the broker.
    C. subpoena the broker for a hearing.
    D. suspend the broker's license until the complaint is resolved.

111. The Missouri Real Estate Commission, having grounds to believe a licensee may have violated the law, may file suit in

    A. only the U.S. District Court.
    B. only the appeals court.
    C. only the county where the act has been committed.
    D. any court of competent jurisdiction.

112. Members of the Missouri Real Estate Commission have heard rumors that a broker is violating the license law. May the Missouri Real Estate Commission investigate the broker?

    A. Yes, but the Missouri Real Estate Commission is limited to investigating only the incident that sparked the rumor
    B. Yes, because no complaint is necessary for the Missouri Real Estate Commission to investigate a licensee
    C. No, because no complaint has been filed by either a licensee or the general public
    D. No, because there has been no allegation of illegal conduct

113. Who of the following requires a license?

    A. Attorney transferring real estate for a client
    B. Auctioneer employed by an owner
    C. Person selling his or her neighbor's property for a small fee
    D. Owner transferring his or her own property

114. A licensed salesperson would most likely be a(n)

    A. independent contractor or subassociate.
    B. employee or consultant.
    C. employee or independent contractor.
    D. subassociate or consultant.

115. An independent contractor is selling easements for several utility companies. Would she require a real estate license?

    A. Yes, because she is an employee of a utility company
    B. Yes, because as an independent contractor she is required to have a license
    C. No, because utility easements are in gross
    D. No, because she is an employee

116. A broker is considering incorporating his real estate business. If he does so, which of the following would require a license?

    A. Corporation only
    B. Broker only
    C. Corporation, the broker, and the stockholders
    D. Corporation and the broker

117. Several individuals want to form a corporation to operate a real estate business. Each of these individuals will be officers of the corporation. Which is true for a corporation to receive a broker's license?

    A. All brokers licensed under the corporation must be officers of the corporation.
    B. Each corporate officer involved in the brokerage business must have an active broker-officer's license.
    C. Each corporate officer must have an active broker-salesperson's license.
    D. When the license is issued to the corporation, the officers will no longer require individual licenses.

118. An inactive partner of a real estate business is required to have a

    A. broker-partner license.
    B. broker-officer license.
    C. broker-associate license.
    D. No license is required.

119. A person applying for the broker's school must have

    A. been actively licensed as a salesperson for at least one year.
    B. permission of the sponsoring broker.
    C. passed the salesperson's exam.
    D. permission of the sponsoring broker and the Missouri Real Estate Commission.

120. All of the following are grounds for the Missouri Real Estate Commission to refuse to issue a license EXCEPT

    A. conviction of obtaining money under false pretenses.
    B. fraud in the application for a license.
    C. bankruptcy.
    D. revocation of a previous license.

121. To receive a credit for satisfactory completion, a student must be present for what percentage of the prelicense course?

    A. 75 percent
    B. 90 percent
    C. 100 percent
    D. The percentage the school deems necessary

122. Which of the following requires a real estate license?

    A. Resident manager who collects rent on behalf of a building owner
    B. A company that, for a fee, matches individuals from different parts of the country who want to exchange properties and that assists them in doing so
    C. An employee selling property for a railroad
    D. Executor selling a decedent's building

123. If engaged in real estate activities, which of the following are exempt from the real estate licensing requirement?

    A. Attorneys at law
    B. Appraisers
    C. Associations, partnerships, corporations
    D. Persons who receive a fee for giving a broker a real estate referral

124. The office manager for a local real estate firm is responsible for the following activities: coordinating the flow of paperwork through the office, preparing forms and advertising copy, and hiring and supervising clerical personnel. The office manager is

    A. violating the license law.
    B. required to have a broker's license.
    C. required to have a salesperson's license.
    D. exempt from real estate licensing requirements.

125. In Missouri, all of the following are requirements for obtaining a broker's license EXCEPT

    A. having successfully completed 48 hours of approved real estate courses.
    B. being at least 18 years of age.
    C. having been actively engaged as a licensed salesperson for at least three years.
    D. being of good moral character.

126. A person successfully completed her real estate education requirement on November 1, 2000. What is the latest date on which she may apply for a salesperson's license?

    A. December 31, 2000
    B. May 31, 2001
    C. October 31, 2001
    D. November 1, 2002

127. Three weeks before N begins his real estate prelicense class, he offers to help his neighbor sell her house. The neighbor agrees to pay N a 5 percent commission. An offer is accepted while N is taking the class and closes the day before N passes the examination and applies for his salesperson's license. The neighbor refuses to pay N the agreed commission. Can N sue to recover payment?

    A. Yes; because N was formally enrolled in a course of study intended to result in a real estate license at the time an offer was procured and accepted, the commission agreement is binding.
    B. No; because a real estate salesperson must have a permanent office in which his or her license is displayed in order to collect a commission from a seller.
    C. Yes; because the statute of frauds forbids recovery on an oral agreement for the conveyance of real property, Missouri law permits enforcement of an oral commission contract under these facts.
    D. No; because state law prohibits lawsuits to collect commissions unless the injured party is a licensed broker and the license was in effect before the agreement was reached.

128. An applicant for a real estate license in Missouri must

    A. have completed at least two years of college.
    B. be at least 18 years old.
    C. not have been convicted of a felony within five years before applying.
    D. show proof of passing the license examination any time up to six months prior to the application.

129. How many hours of continuing education are required to renew a real estate license?

    A. 6
    B. 9
    C. 12
    D. 15

130. A salesperson attended a luncheon where a speaker gave a one-hour presentation on real estate financing. The speaker was a Missouri Real Estate Commission-approved continuing education instructor. Could the salespeople attending the luncheon receive continuing education credit for the presentation?

    A. Yes, if the approved instructor spoke for the entire luncheon period
    B. Yes, if the material and instructor qualifications were submitted to the Missouri Real Estate Commission for its approval
    C. No, because the presentation was during a luncheon
    D. No, because the presentation was not at least three hours in duration

131. A licensee attended three elective continuing education courses for six hours each. The licensee may

    A. use 3 hours for the current renewal period and carry forward 15 hours into the next renewal period.
    B. use 9 hours for this renewal period and carry forward 9 hours into the next renewal period.
    C. use 9 hours for this renewal period and lose the other 9 hours.
    D. use 12 hours for this renewal period and lose the other 6 hours.

132. Salesperson O has been licensed for ten years and another salesperson N received her license within the last year. What, if any, are their continuing education or "post-license" education requirements for license renewal?

    A. O has no requirements, but N is required to complete continuing education to renew her license.
    B. O is required to complete continuing education to renew his license, but N is not.
    C. Both salespeople are required to complete education to renew their licenses.
    D. Neither salesperson is required to complete continuing education to renew their licenses.

133. What are the responsibilities of the Missouri Real Estate Commission and a licensee regarding license renewal?

    A. Each licensee will be sent a renewal notice by certified mail.
    B. If a licensee does not receive a renewal notice, there will be a 30-day grace period.
    C. Each licensee must send in the appropriate renewal application and renewal fee.
    D. Renewal is automatic unless the licensee is notified otherwise.

134. A salesperson does not renew her license. Three months later she wants to reinstate her license. She would be required to

    A. pay $400 plus the license fee.
    B. pay $200 plus the license fee.
    C. pay $150 plus the license fee.
    D. complete the prelicense course and pass the salesperson's examination.

135. When must real estate salespersons renew their licenses in Missouri?

    A. by March 31 of every odd-numbered year
    B. by June 30 of every even-numbered year
    C. by September 30 of each even-numbered year
    D. by January 31 of every odd-numbered year

136. To renew a license in Missouri, a salesperson or broker must

    A. pay a fee of $225 only.
    B. be actively participating in the real estate business.
    C. have completed six hours of continuing education in the last two years: three hours in real estate law and three hours in fair housing.
    D. have completed 12 hours of continuing education in the last two years.

137. In Missouri, licenses are renewed

    A. annually, in the month issued.
    B. every two years in the month of the licensee's birthday.
    C. on January 1 of each even-numbered year.
    D. June 30 of each even-numbered year for brokers and September 30 of each even numbered year for salespeople.

138. Routine services that do not create an agency relationship are referred to as

    A. transaction brokerage.
    B. representation.
    C. ministerial acts.
    D. customer service.

139. An unlicensed secretary is the only person in the broker's office when another broker calls requesting information on property listed with her broker. The secretary may

    A. give the broker the sales price and address of the property.
    B. take the broker's name and telephone number and have a licensee return the call.
    C. give the requested information because the broker is not a member of the general public.
    D. mail the broker the requested information.

140. In Missouri, an unlicensed real estate assistant may perform all of the following activities EXCEPT

    A. compute commission checks.
    B. assemble legal documents required for a closing.
    C. explain simple contract documents to prospective buyers.
    D. prepare and distribute flyers and promotional materials.

141. Regarding licensing and duties of personal real estate assistants in Missouri, they

    A. must be licensed.
    B. may insert factual information into form contracts under the employing broker's supervision and approval.
    C. may independently host open houses and home show booths.
    D. must be unlicensed individuals; licensees must be either salespeople or associate brokers.

142. A broker's unlicensed assistant worked late nights and weekends to help ensure the successful closing of a difficult transaction. The assistant's extra work included making several phone calls to the prospective buyers, encouraging them to accept the seller's counteroffer. Largely because of the assistant's efforts, the sale went through with no problem. Now the broker wants to pay the assistant a percentage of the commission, "because the assistant has really earned it." Under Missouri law, the broker may

    A. compensate the assistant in the form of a commission under the circumstances described here.
    B. not pay the assistant a cash commission but is permitted to make a gift of tangible personal property.
    C. not pay a commission to the assistant under the facts presented here. They are both in violation of rules regarding unlicensed assistants.
    D. pay a commission to the assistant only if the assistant is an independent contractor.

143. Posting a "For Sale" sign on a property without the owner's permission would NOT lead to which of the following by the Missouri Real Estate Commission?

    A. Criminal prosecution
    B. A fine by the Missouri Real Estate Commission
    C. Civil damages
    D. Disciplinary action by the Missouri Real Estate Commission

144. A salesperson told a buyer that "the window air conditioner stays with the property" without confirming this with the seller. The buyer purchased the property and, after closing, the seller removed the air conditioner. Under the Missouri license law, the

   A. salesperson would be required by the Missouri Real Estate Commission to pay for the air conditioner.
   B. Missouri Real Estate Commission could automatically revoke the salesperson's license.
   C. Missouri Real Estate Commission may take disciplinary action against the salesperson and his broker.
   D. buyer would have to look to the seller for relief.

145. A nonresident broker applying for a Missouri license would pay a license fee of

   A. $40 per licensure period for a salesperson.
   B. $80 per licensure period for a broker.
   C. $50 per licensure period.
   D. the same amount a Missouri resident would pay in the nonresident's state.

146. Chapter 339 is known as

   A. the law of agency.
   B. Missouri license law.
   C. Missouri Real Estate Commission rules and regulations.
   D. Hulse vs. Criger.

147. The purpose of the license law is to

   A. provide a means for enforcement and for disciplining licensees.
   B. increase revenues for the state.
   C. control the real estate business.
   D. protect the public.

148. In applying for a real estate license, an applicant must

   A. make a written application.
   B. have at least 12 months' apprenticeship.
   C. make application within 12 months after completing the prelicense course.
   D. be at least 21 years of age.

149. A salesperson wanted to obtain a broker's license, but has an unresolved complaint pending against her. In this situation, the salesperson

   A. may not apply for a broker's license until the complaint is resolved.
   B. must place her license on inactive status until the complaint is resolved.
   C. may apply for a broker's license.
   D. may take the broker's prelicense course and the broker's examination, but may not apply for the broker's license.

150. If an applicant is denied a license, the Missouri Real Estate Commission must

   A. notify the applicant in writing, stating the reason for the denial.
   B. turn the case over to the Missouri Attorney General.
   C. advise the applicant of his or her right to file a complaint with HUD.
   D. inform the applicant in writing within ten days.

151. An application for a salesperson's license requires the signatures of

   A. the salesperson only.
   B. the broker only.
   C. both the broker and salesperson.
   D. the broker, salesperson, and Missouri Real Estate Commission.

152. A broker has a change of home address. How long does the broker have to notify the Missouri Real Estate Commission?

    A. 10 days
    B. 30 days
    C. 20 days
    D. At the time of license renewal

153. An unlicensed person sells property of another for a fee. What may the Missouri Real Estate Commission do?

    A. Require the person to obtain a real estate license
    B. File for a restraining order in a court of competent jurisdiction
    C. File criminal charges against the person
    D. Fine the person for committing a misdemeanor

154. All of the following statements regarding the Missouri Real Estate Commission are true EXCEPT that the

    A. state association of REALTORS® selects members of the commission.
    B. commission makes and enforces the rules by which all real estate licensees must abide.
    C. examinations that must be taken by all applicants for real estate licensing are administered by an independent testing company.
    D. operation of the commission's activities is administered by an executive director specifically hired for that purpose.

155. The on-site property manager for Acme Apartments is responsible for negotiating leases for the apartments. In this position, the on-site manager

    A. must have a salesperson's license.
    B. must have a broker's license.
    C. is exempt from the licensing requirements.
    D. is violating the license law.

156. All of the following are exempt from the provisions of the Missouri Real Estate Commission rules and regulations EXCEPT a(n)

    A. property owner who sells or leases his or her own property.
    B. individual who receives compensation for procuring prospective buyers or renters of real estate.
    C. individual who is employed as a resident property manager.
    D. licensed attorney at law.

157. What are the licensing requirements for an individual who wishes to sell his or her own property?

    A. An owner does not need a real estate license to sell his or her own property.
    B. In Missouri, anyone who sells real property must first have a real estate license issued by the real estate commission.
    C. The individual may obtain a temporary real estate license to legally sell his or her own house.
    D. The owner may sell his or her house without obtaining a real estate license only if the owner is a licensed attorney.

158. Which of the following is a requirement to obtain a real estate salesperson's license in Missouri?

    A. Successful completion of 12 credit hours of real estate law, investments, finance, and appraisal
    B. An associate degree or certificate in real estate from an accredited college, university, or proprietary school
    C. United States citizenship
    D. Successful completion of a course of 60 classroom hours at a school accredited by the Missouri Real Estate Commission

159. Which of the following situations would qualify for the CE requirement in Missouri?

    A. 12-hour course on using real estate office spreadsheet programs, offered by a local community college
    B. six-hour commission-approved course on managing agricultural property, offered by an approved CE sponsor
    C. Retaking and passing the licensing exam
    D. Teaching a prelicense course several evenings a week

160. What is the expiration date of every salesperson's license in Missouri?

    A. January 31 of every even-numbered year
    B. March 31 of each odd-numbered year
    C. October 31 of each odd-numbered year
    D. September 30 of each even-numbered year

161. A person must be licensed as a real estate broker or salesperson if that person is

    A. selling his or her house.
    B. buying a house for his or her personal use.
    C. engaging in the real estate business.
    D. constructing houses.

162. All of the following are title search methods commonly used by an attorney in Missouri EXCEPT a

    A. land court certificate.
    B. title search and opinion.
    C. certificate of title.
    D. full abstract.

163. A broker wants to transfer her license from inactive status to active status after being inactive for nine months. What would she have to do?

    A. Satisfactorily complete the prelicense course within six months prior to transfer
    B. Satisfactorily complete 12 hours of continuing education
    C. Pay a delinquent fee
    D. Pass the real estate examination

164. A broker has had his license on inactive status for two years and now wants to practice real estate. He must send in the renewal fee and transfer form, and complete

    A. the prelicense course.
    B. the prelicense course and pass the examination.
    C. his continuing education.
    D. his continuing education and prelicense course.

165. Which is required of a licensee with a license on inactive status?

   A. The biennial renewal fee must be paid.
   B. The licensee must complete continuing education.
   C. The licensee must complete the prelicense course.
   D. The licensee must transfer to active status within six months after placing his or her license on inactive status.

166. May a person with a "work permit" from the Missouri Real Estate Commission solicit new listings and contracts?

   A. No, because he or she is not licensed.
   B. No, because he or she may only prospect for new customers until his or her permanent license is issued.
   C. Yes, if given permission by the Missouri Real Estate Commission
   D. Yes, because he or she has a license

167. A broker died and a salesperson was granted a temporary broker license by the Missouri Real Estate Commission. What may the salesperson do?

   A. Solicit buyers for existing listings, but may not solicit new listings
   B. Solicit buyers for existing listings and solicit new listings
   C. Close the transactions that are under contract and solicit buyers for existing listings
   D. Arrange for closing the transactions that are under contract, but may not solicit buyers for existing listings and may not solicit new listings

168. A broker who is a member of a franchise must file a copy of the franchise agreement with the

   A. city.
   B. state.
   C. county.
   D. attorney general.

169. A broker is a member of a real estate franchise. Which of the following is true?

   A. The broker must register the franchise with the local Board of REALTORS®.
   B. The president of the franchise company is responsible for the broker's actions.
   C. Advertising must clearly reveal that the broker owns and operates the real estate firm.
   D. The franchise name may not be used in an advertisement.

170. A broker who is a member of a franchise must include a statement that the franchiser is not liable for the broker's actions on any of the following EXCEPT

   A. listing agreements.
   B. contracts.
   C. closing statements.
   D. advertising.

171. At the closing of a transaction the buyer asks the salesperson a question that concerns a point of law that the salesperson knows. The salesperson should

   A. refer the question to his or her broker.
   B. refer the buyer to a real estate attorney.
   C. answer the question because he or she knows the answer.
   D. advise the buyer to consult with the buyer's attorney.

172. A salesperson is showing property to a buyer. They passed a home with a "For Sale by Owner" sign in the yard. The buyer wants to see the property. What should the salesperson do?

   A. Stop and ask the owner if she can show the property to the buyer
   B. Go to a nearby service station and call the property owner to set an appointment to show the property
   C. Tell the buyer she will have to contact the property owner and make the proper arrangements in order to be able to show the buyer the property
   D. Tell the buyer she may not show the property under any circumstance

173. License fees are payable by

   A. cash by registered mail.
   B. company check only.
   C. personal check, money order, or cashier's check.
   D. anything of material value.

174. A home listed with one brokerage was sold, under a cobroker agreement, by a salesperson from another real estate brokerage. The selling salesperson is closing the transaction with both brokers in attendance. The closing statement is signed by the

   A. cobroker.
   B. cobroker's salesperson.
   C. listing broker.
   D. listing broker's salesperson.

175. A home listed with a brokerage was sold, under a cobroker agreement, by a salesperson from a different brokerage. The selling salesperson is closing the transaction with both brokers in attendance. The responsibility for ensuring delivery of the closing statement to both buyer and seller rests with the

   A. cobroker.
   B. cobroker's salesperson.
   C. listing broker.
   D. listing broker's salesperson.

176. A listing salesperson is a friend of both the buyer and seller. The buyer and seller both wanted her to close the transaction for them. May the salesperson do this?

   A. Yes, provided the closing is under direct supervision of the salesperson's broker
   B. Yes, because the buyer and seller knew the salesperson and requested she close
   C. No, because a salesperson is not allowed to close a real estate transaction
   D. No, because the salesperson is a friend of both the buyer and seller

177. A listing broker arranges for a title company to provide title insurance for the real estate transaction and close the transaction. There are errors on the closing statement, and the title company fails to provide the buyer and seller with a copy of the closing statement. Who is responsible under the Rules and Regulations of the Missouri Real Estate Commission?

   A. The listing broker
   B. The title company
   C. Both the listing broker and the title company
   D. Neither the listing broker nor the title company

178. Under what circumstances may a salesperson close a real estate transaction?

   A. Under the direct supervision of the listing broker
   B. Under the direct supervision of his or her broker
   C. Under the direct supervision of any broker
   D. Under no circumstance because only brokers may close real estate transactions

179. In Missouri, the responsibility for preparing any promissory notes involved in a closing belongs to the

   A. seller's broker.
   B. settlement attorney.
   C. lender.
   D. buyer.

180. A sales contract is signed on May 1. Closing takes place on June 10, and the deed of trust is recorded on June 15. The borrower's first payment is due on August 30. When is the most typical date that the broker will receive his or her commission check?

   A. May 1
   B. June 10
   C. June 15
   D. August 30

181. A broker or salesperson may perform all of the following in preparation for the closing EXCEPT

   A. maintain a time schedule and provide net data.
   B. explain closing procedures to both buyer and seller and anticipate decision-making alternatives.
   C. coordinate inspections and deliver documents and escrow monies to the appropriate attorney.
   D. conduct any title searches that might be required.

182. Which of the following legal descriptions is used in Missouri?

   A. Metes and bounds
   B. Government rectangular survey system
   C. Recorded plats
   D. All of the above

183. In Missouri, an individual may enter into legally enforceable contracts (with no exceptions) when he or she reaches the age of

   A. 16.
   B. 18.
   C. 19.
   D. 21.

184. If a minor enters into a contract in Missouri, what is the statutory period within which he or she may legally void the contract after reaching the age of majority?

   A. 6 months
   B. 1 year
   C. The contract may be voided only up to the date when the minor reaches the age of majority; after that date, the contract is binding.
   D. There is no statutory period.

185. A broker hired a manager to manage an apartment complex. The manager showed units, executed leases, and maintained and made improvements to the property. Is the manager required to have a real estate license?

    A. Yes, because the manager made improvements to the land
    B. Yes, because the manager showed and leased the property
    C. No, because leasing does not fall under the definition of brokerage
    D. No, because property managers doing these activities are exempt from licensure

186. Which would LEAST likely be in a property management agreement?

    A. Description of the property
    B. Exact amount of rent for each unit
    C. Property manager's compensation
    D. Exact documents that must be provided by the manager to the owner

187. A couple has signed a lease containing a provision to waive their rights to the interest earned from the security deposit. This provision is

    A. unenforceable, thus making the lease invalid.
    B. unenforceable, but the lease is still valid.
    C. enforceable because all parties agreed to it.
    D. enforceable only for the term of the lease.

188. When should a landlord first present rules and regulations to tenants of leased property?

    A. When a tenant first violates them
    B. When a tenant requests them
    C. At any time during the rental agreement
    D. At the time a tenant enters into the rental agreement or at the time the rules or regulations are adopted

189. During a crime wave, a tenant decides to install a burglar alarm in a rented house. Does the tenant need to inform the landlord?

    A. No, because the tenant has full right of possession during the lease
    B. No, because only tenants in multiunit apartment buildings are required to inform a landlord about a security system
    C. Yes, but the tenant must also give the landlord instructions and passwords
    D. Yes, but the cost of the system may be deducted from the rent

190. With regard to the responsibilities of the Missouri Real Estate Commission and the administrative hearing commission, the

   A. Missouri Real Estate Commission must send all complaints to the administrative hearing commission.
   B. Missouri Real Estate Commission may revoke a license, without further hearings, after a Missouri Real Estate Commission investigation reveals there is a legitimate complaint against the licensee.
   C. administrative hearing commission must find the licensee guilty before the Missouri Real Estate Commission may revoke a license.
   D. administrative hearing commission may make no recommendations to the Missouri Real Estate Commission as to the disciplinary action to be taken against a licensee found guilty of violating the law.

191. The administrative hearing commission may

   A. investigate a complaint.
   B. impose a penalty against a licensee found guilty of violating the law.
   C. conduct hearings to determine the guilt or innocence of a licensee charged with a violation and make recommendations to the real estate commission as to punishment.
   D. take control of a real estate business when the owner is found guilty of a violation of the law.

192. A licensee has been found guilty of a license law violation and has had his license revoked. He may appeal his conviction and penalty to the

   A. real estate commission.
   B. administrative hearing commission.
   C. circuit court.
   D. Missouri Attorney General.

193. The Missouri Real Estate Commission has refused to issue a license to an applicant who has completed all the necessary requirements for a license. The applicant may appeal to the

   A. real estate commission.
   B. administrative hearing commission.
   C. circuit court.
   D. Missouri Attorney General.

194. How soon should deeds of conveyance be recorded after closing?

   A. As soon as possible
   B. One business day
   C. Three business days
   D. One month

195. To be eligible for recording in Missouri, a document must be

   A. in any language.
   B. witnessed by two persons who are not affected by the document.
   C. acknowledged.
   D. drawn up by an attorney.

196. From a strictly legal standpoint, real property taxes become a lien on the property as of the

   A. first day of the year.
   B. thirtieth day from the due date.
   C. date of assessment.
   D. date a foreclosure suit is filed and recorded.

197. Properties exempt from general real estate taxes include all of the following EXCEPT

   A. cemeteries.
   B. federal government buildings.
   C. housing owned by a disabled veteran.
   D. private schools.

198. In Missouri, real estate taxes become a lien on the property on

A. January 1.
B. June 30.
C. July 1.
D. December 31.

199. A husband and wife, who own their home as tenants by the entireties, obtain a divorce. At that time, in Missouri, the tenancy by the entireties

A. extinguishes and becomes a tenancy in common.
B. continues until one of them dies.
C. extinguishes and becomes a tenancy at sufferance.
D. reverts to common interest ownership.

200. Unless stated to the contrary in a deed, ownership of land by a married couple is assumed to be by

A. severalty.
B. joint tenancy.
C. tenancy in common.
D. tenancy by the entirety.

Answer Key

1. A. The broker earned the commission because he procured a ready, willing, and able buyer on terms agreeable to the seller.

2. D. If both parties agree in writing, then the brokerage can represent both parties. Agency is about relationships; how the agent is paid is a separate issue.

3. C. When working for the seller, a subagent is required to confirm the brokerage relationship in writing to the buyer no later than when the buyer signs an offer to purchase property.

4. B. If the buyer and seller have not entered into any signed agency agreements or sale contracts, a broker could assist the parties with negotiation and completion of the contract and close this transaction as a transaction broker. In this situation, the broker would not represent either party. The broker simply facilitates the transaction.

5. A. In this situation, "representation" indicates an agency relationship with each party. The commission splits between brokers are not relevant to agency representation.

6. C. A transaction broker represents neither the buyer nor the seller and may not act as an agent for either.

7. C. A transaction broker is responsible for presenting all offers in a timely manner but is not an agent for the buyer or seller and may not reveal to the seller any motivating factors of the buyer.

8. C. A transaction broker does not represent either party, buyer or seller, in a transaction.

9. B. Of course, the original listing agent is now free to represent the buyer. The original agent no longer has an agency relationship with the seller. However, confidential information must remain confidential forever. Agents must always disclose information about the physical condition of the property.

10. A. Acceptance of a referral fee or kickback is a violation of RESPA and the salesperson can receive compensation only from their employing brokers.

11. C. The salesperson must indicate that the agency represents the seller. This is not dual agency because the buyer does not wish representation. Any agency agreement must be in writing.

12. C. Buyers can enter into an exclusive-right-to-buy agreement, but it must be clearly identified. Both the broker and buyer must sign the contract.

13. A. The buyer limited agent contract is an employment contract. Buyer limited agent contracts are definitely regulated, just as listing agreements are. The Missouri Real Estate Commission does not provide forms for use by licensees.

14. B. The listing does not have to be accompanied by a qualified expert's report of the property condition. It must state the exact fee the broker will earn (either a flat fee or a percentage), must be in writing, and must be signed by both broker and seller. The seller must receive a true copy of the listing agreement after signing it.

15. C. Both parties must give their signed, contractual consent to the dual compensation.

16. A. The seller must give permission for subagency or transaction brokerage. The buyer has indicated that the buyer does not desire representation. Companies must have a cobroker agreement in order to show each other's listings (which may include MLS).

17. A. While a seller property condition disclosure statement is not mandated by Missouri law, the statement should be delivered to the buyer prior to the buyer's making a written offer. The buyer needs this information in order to make an informed offer.

18. B. A licensee in the state of Missouri must disclose that he or she is a licensee in any transaction of buying, selling, or renting property. A licensee is not required to charge a commission, inform his or her broker, or sell the property at full market value.

19. A. A licensee has the duty to disclose all material facts to all involved parties in the sale of the property. A crack in the basement may be a structural problem; therefore, this must be disclosed. The licensee could face problems by not disclosing or by hiding the problem.

20. A. A licensee must disclose any future interest in buying or selling property. His potential marriage and ownership of this property requires disclosure not only of being a licensee but also of future interest.

21. B. A licensee, whether the license is on active or inactive status, must disclose this fact to a buyer or seller whether purchasing property in state or out of state.

22. D. A licensee must disclose any adverse material fact in the sale of property, whether residential or commercial. Transaction brokers must disclose adverse material facts of which they have actual knowledge. Licensees acting as agents must disclose material facts of which they had actual knowledge or of which they should have known. Other factors, such as written communications, past and present income, and unseen structural defects are not relied upon as material facts.

23. C. This disclosure must be made so that buyers understand that they are not being represented. Buyers do not have to be represented to work with the seller's agent. Such disclosure must be confirmed in writing prior to or upon their execution of an offer to purchase.

24. D. The salesperson will have to inform the owner in writing that the salesperson is a licensee. The salesperson does not have to resign or notify the real estate commission, and he or she should not use a third party.

25. A. The buyer can sue the broker in civil court for the failure to disclose a material fact. In addition, the buyer could file a complaint with the real estate commission for a violation of the license law. Both actions are valid, regardless of the fact that the buyer did not ask about the roof.

26. A. The Missouri Broker Disclosure Form must be delivered to the consumer at the first practicable opportunity when working with that consumer. The Rules and Regulations of the Missouri Real Estate Commission also state that the form must be given "in any event…upon obtaining any personal or financial information or before the signing of a brokerage service agreement, whichever occurs first."

27. C. The licensee's disclosure violated the fiduciary duties owed to the tenant by violating the duty of confidentiality to the tenant who hired the licensee. Representation is determined by who does the hiring, not who pays the fee.

28. B. The salesperson has properly disclosed his or her agency relationship. The salesperson must present the Missouri Broker Disclosure Form to a customer at the first practicable opportunity.

29. A. The salesperson may provide comparable market data to the seller and buyer. The dual agent may not disclose the buyer's financial qualifications to the seller, disclose to the buyer that the seller will accept less than the listing price, or disclose to the seller that the buyer will pay more than the offering price.

30. B. The brokerage relationship with a seller must be determined and agreed to before performing any brokerage activities as a seller's agent.

31. C. The seller and buyer must be informed of the situation and agree to the broker's representing both of them.

32. D. Commission rates are always negotiable between the seller and the broker. The real estate commission may revoke a license if the licensee has been convicted of a felony or for false advertising. Commingling of funds is prohibited.

33. D. Depositing a buyer's down payment into one's own bank account would be commingling of personal and client's funds, a prohibited practice. A salesperson may enter into dual agency agreements. A salesperson may represent a buyer. Most real estate brokers prefer an exclusive-listing agreement.

34. B. Depositing earnest money into the firm's escrow account is proper conduct. Grounds for suspension or revocation include but are not limited to: mental incompetency, cheating on the licensing exam, and displaying a "For Sale" sign without the owner's consent.

35. A. The Missouri Real Estate Commission may or may not issue a person a license if the person has been convicted of embezzlement. The commission will take a look at all circumstances surrounding this situation before making a decision. The person may attend prelicense school, take the exam, and apply for a license.

36. C. A broker may pay a referral fee to a salesperson licensed with the broker, another broker in the state of Missouri, or a broker in another state.

37. D. A salesperson must be licensed in Missouri to sell property in Missouri for another and for compensation.

38. C. This is an example of writing dual contracts and is expressly forbidden. The broker would be subject to disciplinary procedures for doing this.

39. D. A licensee must have a signed listing agreement with the sellers to place a "For Sale" sign on property. Placing a "For Sale" sign on property not listed is a violation, and the licensee may be disciplined for false advertising.

40. D. A licensee may continue to do business as usual while an investigation is taking place. The commission will investigate and then decide what action to take.

41. D. The Missouri Real Estate Commission may not imprison a violator of the rules and regulations. A violation is a Class B misdemeanor, a licensee may be subject to fines from a court of law, and a licensee may be subject to civil liability to the aggrieved person.

42. A. The Missouri Real Estate Commission publishes a summary report of the administrative hearing commission decisions relating to violations of the license law and other laws. The administrative hearing commission does not set the penalties when a licensee is found guilty; the Missouri Real Estate Commission sets the penalties. Information gained in investigations is private.

43. B. The law specifically states that a person selling real estate for another and for compensation must be licensed. In this case, this person would be guilty of a Class B misdemeanor for the violation.

44. C. Brokers are not to be parties to dual contracts for the purpose of obtaining a larger loan.

45. A. As with all advertising, "For Sale" signs must contain the broker's name and phone number. A salesperson cannot advertise property in the salesperson's name alone.

46. C. In a guaranteed sales plan, all information about the plan must be disclosed in advertising. The commission does not need to approve the advertising.

47. D. A salesperson selling his or her own home and not listing it for sale must disclose in advertising his or her licensee status--in this case, "Owner/Salesperson" on the "For Sale" sign.

48. A. A broker is required to have the broker's name and phone number on all advertising signs of listed property. Putting the broker's name on the signs indicates that a brokerage is involved and does not lead to charges of "blind" advertising.

49. A. After obtaining the owner's permission, the broker may erect a "For Sale" sign on the property. If the owner requests that no "For Sale" sign be placed on the property, this is a legal request and must be followed.

50. C. Net listings are illegal in Missouri because of potential conflict of interest for the broker.

51. C. The broker accepted an illegal net listing. This is a good example of the conflict of interest that a net listing provokes. The broker was not working in the best interest of his client.

52. C. The Missouri Real Estate Commission will not get involved in disputes between brokers concerning commissions.

53. C. The Missouri Real Estate Commission will not become involved in disputes between licensees concerning commissions.

54. C. The listing commission is always paid to the listing broker. The listing broker can then split the commission as agreed upon.

55. C. A broker in Missouri may pay a commission to a salesperson licensed with the broker, another broker in the state of Missouri, or a broker in another state.

56. D. Commissions are always negotiable between the principal and the agent. Commissions are not determined by law, by the Missouri Real Estate Commission, or by a group of local brokers.

57. A. Commissions are always negotiable between the principal and the agent and are not determined by custom or law. The commission may not be deducted from the earnest money deposit or shared with an unlicensed party.

58. B. The earnest money must be paid to the escrow agent specified in the sales contract, whether a listing broker, buyer's agent, title company or other entity. If the earnest money check is to be made payable to the listing broker, the salesperson must give it to the broker immediately.

59. B. This is an example of commingling and would lead to disciplinary action against the broker.

60. A. Earnest money checks must be made payable to the broker and delivered to the broker immediately.

61. D. A broker is required to hold earnest money in the escrow account until all parties to the contract agree on how the money is to be disbursed and sign an agreement of release.

62. C. The broker's escrow account, name, and number of the account must be disclosed to the Missouri Real Estate Commission and must be in the state of Missouri or, with the Missouri Real Estate Commission's permission, in a bank in an adjoining state.

63. C. Any request past the ten days the broker has to deposit the earnest money requires seller approval.

64. C. All money received for rent must be deposited into the property management escrow account.

65. D. Money for maintenance and current rent is deposited into the property management escrow account.

66. D. Other people's money, such as earnest money and security deposits, must be deposited within ten banking days after the final signature is obtained.

67. C. The broker is in violation of regulations for handling escrow funds by improperly using funds from one property to make repairs on another.

68. B. On contracts approved by the broker's counsel, the blanks may be filled in by licensees. Real estate licensees who are not lawyers must be careful to avoid any appearance of the unauthorized practice of law.

69. B. A real estate broker and his or her salespeople may use standardized forms, but they must have been prepared or approved by the broker's attorney or by the counsel for a trade association of which the broker is a member or associate member, or by a Missouri state or local bar association.

70. A. All agreements signed between a broker and a principal, including a listing agreement, must have a copy given to the principal at the time of signing.

71. D. Because there is no buyer at the time of the listing, a buyer signature could not be obtained. Also, when a buyer is procured, he or she is not requested to sign the listing. Listing agreements may not have automatic extensions, must have specific expiration dates, and a copy must be given to the seller at the time of signing.

72. B. An adequate description, such as the property address, is required, but not the legal description. Listings must have an asking price and a definable broker fee. Listings must have a definite termination date.

73. B. Listings must contain a definite termination date, and rollover extensions are not permitted under Missouri law.

74. B. Listings must have a definite termination date. Including a specific termination date would be following the state law. State law does not address the issue of whether or not to include a broker protection clause. Commission rates are required to avoid net listings; there must be a specific termination date.

75. D. The licensee is obligated to give the seller signing the listing a legible, signed, true, and correct copy. Other brokers are not required to participate in marketing. Advertising or numbering the files is not required.

76. B. The listing agreement may be canceled but the seller may be responsible for time and expenses. The Missouri Real Estate Commission will not be involved.

77. A. A broker-salesperson must work for another broker. If a broker-salesperson wants to work for himself, then he must complete a transfer form, pay the required fee, and send it to the Missouri Real Estate Commission requesting a transfer to a broker-individual license. One would not need to pass another exam or attend school.

78. A. A salesperson may also auction property for an owner but is not allowed to accept compensation from any other broker, owner of listed property, or another salesperson.

79. C. Salespeople may accept compensation only from the broker they are licensed with.

80. B. A salesperson is an agent for the broker he or she is working with and is responsible to that broker by contractual agreement. Unless working under a designated agency agreement, a salesperson is not the primary agent of the buyer or the seller, and is never the agent of another salesperson. The broker or brokerage is the person or entity that is the agent.

81. B. Salespeople may collect compensation only from their employing brokers.

82. A. A salesperson may be licensed with only one broker.

83. D. The broker-salesperson acted improperly. A broker-salesperson may collect a fee only from his or her employing broker.

84. D. If the broker's license is suspended or revoked, all the salespersons' and broker-salespersons' licenses are returned to the Missouri Real Estate Commission until "hired" by a new broker.

85. A. A broker-salesperson may manage a branch office. A licensee must hold a broker's license to manage or own a real estate company.

86. D. All licenses must be kept at the office of the licensee and displayed to the public on request.

87. B. A broker must provide to the Missouri Real Estate Commission the addresses of all branch offices and the name of the licensee in charge of each office. Each time a change is made, the broker has ten days to notify the commission of this change.

88. C. Each branch office in Missouri must be named the same as the parent office. The Missouri Real Estate Commission does not assign names for real estate offices.

89. D. Each office must be under the direction of a licensed real estate broker. Brokers can have branch offices, but each office must be under the direction of a licensed real estate broker.

90. D. The old license must be returned to the commission along with proper fee and a form signed by the new broker. The new broker must receive the new license or work permit before the broker-salesperson can start selling.

91. B. The commission must be notified within ten days or the broker risks losing the license. The real estate commission does not have to approve the new location.

92. A. Because this agreement was completed before the broker was contacted, the broker may not be a party to this contract or enter into it after the fact. The buyer and seller should consult with a real estate attorney.

93. A. The broker may not offer a title opinion, which could be unauthorized practice of law. State law requires that these documents be retained for three years. The broker is responsible for the accuracy of the closing statement and should ensure that all terms have been included.

94. A. Most listing agreements provide that the listing broker must produce a ready, willing, and able buyer. Simply having a listing agreement does not ensure a commission. Note that while a civil court action does not require a written listing agreement, the license law does. Failure to secure the written listing agreement may subject the licensee to discipline by the real estate commission.

95. B. State law requires that brokers keep records for at least three years. Brokers are required to have regularly stated hours of operation. There is no requirement that a broker must employ a salesperson. There are many one-person offices.

96. B. Referral fees and kickbacks in the referral of settlement services are illegal under RESPA.

97. C. A salesperson may not accept a fee from anyone other than her employing broker, plus such fees must be disclosed to all parties to the transaction. A fee in return for a referral may be construed as an illegal kickback.

98. D. The broker may say "thank you" to the airline pilot. A broker may pay a referral fee only to another licensed broker.

99. B. On a cooperating agreement between two brokers, the selling broker may work for the listing broker as a subagent and, if so, owes all the fiduciary responsibilities to the seller, as does the listing broker. The presumption of a brokerage relationship is a transaction broker.

100. B. When a licensee transfers to inactive status in the state of Missouri, the licensee is no longer in the real estate business and may not represent buyers and sellers. She may not receive a referral fee from another broker because of the inactive status and does not need a broker to file her inactive license with the commission.

101. B. A broker must have an office and have it open during regularly stated intervals. Brokers may have as many salespeople as they want, may have an office at home, and are not required to have a separate entrance.

102. A. The salesperson must obtain all signatures. Under no circumstances should a licensee sign for a party. This could result in disciplinary action.

103. A. Describing a restaurant as "the best in town" is a matter of personal opinion and is not something a customer would rely on to make a decision to purchase the property. Not telling the buyer of rezoning or a leaking roof or depositing earnest money into one's personal account are violations of the license law.

Missouri Exam Prep

104. A. The brokerage commission must be stated in the listing agreement and is negotiated between the broker and seller. Broker's commissions are not determined by brokers or the Missouri Real Estate Commission.

105. D. A multiple listing is not a type of listing. Exclusive-right-to-sell, exclusive-agency, and open listings must be in writing, indicating a termination date, a specific asking price, and a commission rate.

106. B. The Missouri Real Estate Commission administers the real estate license law. The Missouri Association of REALTORS® is a trade association. HUD is a government agency that supervises housing issues and handles fair housing complaints.

107. A. The governor makes the appointments, but the senate must confirm the appointments. The association of REALTORS® is a trade association, and neither it nor the public elects the commission members.

108. A. The legislature enacts law; the real estate commission is authorized to write rules and regulations that have the force of law. The exam questions are written by an independent testing service and reviewed by the real estate commission. The testing service administers the exams.

109. A. The Missouri Real Estate Commission can investigate on its own discretion.

110. D. The Missouri Real Estate Commission may not arbitrarily suspend the broker's license. Once a complaint is filed, the Missouri Real Estate Commission must investigate the complaint, send the complaint to the administrative hearing commission, and then, if the licensee is found guilty, it may suspend the license, depending on the severity of the violation. They may pay expenses and fees to witnesses involved, subpoena business records, and subpoena the broker for hearings.

111. D. If a licensee is suspected of violating the license law, the Missouri Real Estate Commission may seek a stop order from any court of competent jurisdiction in the county where the licensee resides or the violation is being committed.

112. B. The Missouri Real Estate Commission may investigate a licensee anytime for any reason upon its own motion to do so. No complaint needs to be filed from any person or entity for the Missouri Real Estate Commission to act.

113. C. Any person in the state of Missouri listing or selling property for another and for a commission needs a license. This person would need a license to accept a fee for selling the neighbor's property. An attorney is exempt from licensure, as is an auctioneer employed by an owner or any owner selling his or her own property.

114. C. By license law, a licensee would most likely be an employee or independent contractor.

115. B. An independent contractor selling property for utility companies needs a license because it is for others and for a commission. An employee of the utility company would not need a license to buy and sell property for the utility.

116. D. Entities such as corporations are required to apply and receive a broker's license to establish a real estate company, and the broker is required to have a broker's license.

117. B. Officers active in the real estate corporation, whether managing, listing, or selling, are required to hold broker's licenses. All officers active in the corporation must be licensed brokers for the corporation to obtain its broker's license. A salesperson may not own or manage a real estate company in Missouri.

118. D. Only active partners who are managing, listing, or selling are required to be licensed brokers.

119. C. A person must pass the salesperson's exam before being admitted to the broker program for licensing. There is no one-year requirement to hold a salesperson's license, and no permission from the sponsoring broker or the Missouri Real Estate Commission is needed.

120. C. The Missouri Real Estate Commission will not refuse a license based on bankruptcy. It may refuse a license based on a conviction of obtaining money under false pretense, fraud, or previous license revocation.

121. C. The student must be present for 100 percent of the prelicense course to obtain the certificate.

122. B. Matching individuals for a fee or commission requires a real estate license. The resident manager is specifically exempt from being required to have a real estate license. Court-appointed persons are not required to have a real estate license.

123. A. Attorneys at law are exempt from real estate licensing requirements. Appraisers, associations, partnerships, and corporations, if engaging in real estate activities, must have a real estate license. A person receiving a referral fee from a broker must be licensed.

124. D. The office manager is performing non-real estate activities and is therefore exempt from licensing requirements.

125. C. In Missouri, one may begin the broker program immediately after passing the salesperson exam. The applicant for a broker's exam must have completed 48 hours of approved real estate courses, be at least 18 years of age, and be of good moral character.

126. B. The applicant has until the last day of the sixth month to apply for her license, in this example, May 31, 2001.

127. D. The agent cannot sue the seller; because the injured party must have had an active license at the time the agreement was reached.

128. B. An applicant for a real estate license in Missouri must be 18 years old to apply for a license. No college is required as a prerequisite to real estate licensing. It is up to the Missouri Real Estate Commission to accept or deny a license based on a felony conviction. A person must apply for a license within six months from the last day of prelicense school.

129. C. All licensees, unless exempt, must complete 12 hours of continuing education in the two years previous to license renewal.

130. D. Each continuing education approved course must be at least three hours in duration.

131. C. A licensee is required to attend nine hours of elective courses and three hours of a core course stipulated by the Missouri Real Estate Commission. These were only elective courses, so the licensee will be given credit for only nine elective hours and will need three more hours of a core course. No hours may be carried forward; therefore this licensee will lose the remaining hours.

132. C. Licensees must complete the 12-hour Missouri Real Estate Practice Course in their first renewal period. Licensees must complete nine hours of electives and three hours of a core course after their first renewal and for subsequent renewal periods.

133. C. Each licensee is required to send to the commission, postmarked by each license's renewal date, the renewal application and renewal fee. A licensee will not be sent a notice by certified mail, there is no grace period for renewal, and the renewal is not automatic.

134. C. Delinquent renewal requires a $50-per-month penalty, to a maximum of $200. If continuing education is not completed prior to expiration, then the prelicense course is required, but the licensee will not need to retake the exam.

135. C. Real estate salespeople must renew their licenses by September 30 of each even-numbered year.

136. D. To renew a license in Missouri, licensees must take 12 hours of continuing education within the last two years before the renewal date.

137. D. Licenses must be renewed every two years: June 30 of each even-numbered year for brokers and September 30 of each even-numbered year for salespeople.

138. C. Informational services only are considered "ministerial."

139. B. Unlicensed secretaries may only take messages and have a licensee return the call. They may not hold themselves out to the public as licensees and therefore may not do anything that would require a license, including giving out requested information about a property or mailing requested information concerning properties.

140. C. Only a licensed person may explain simple contract documents to prospective buyers. An unlicensed person may write advertising under the direction of a licensee; do bookkeeping, such as computing commission checks; and perform secretarial work, such as assembling legal documents for closing.

141. B. Administrative work such as inserting factual information into form contracts under the employing broker's supervision and approval does not require licensing because it is done under the supervision of the broker. Personal assistants may be licensed in order to perform more services for the licensee who hired them, but they do not have to be licensed to work as assistants. Only licensed personal assistants may independently host open houses.

142. C. The broker may not pay a commission to the assistant under the facts presented here. Both the broker and assistant are in violation of rules regarding unlicensed assistants. Unlicensed assistants are not permitted to perform the described services.

143. B. The Missouri Real Estate Commission does not fine or imprison, but this action may lead to other disciplinary action.

144. C. The salesperson made a statement breaching the fiduciary responsibility with the seller. The salesperson is in violation and may have a disciplinary hearing. The Missouri Real Estate Commission could not automatically revoke the license, the salesperson would not be required to pay for the air conditioner, and the buyer may look to the broker or the Missouri Real Estate Commission for relief.

145. D. When a nonresident applies for a Missouri license, he or she will pay the same amount a Missouri resident would pay for a nonresident license in that state. The nonresident broker must also sign a consent to suit concerning an escrow account.

146. B. Missouri license law is also known as Chapter 339. Hulse vs. Criger is a Missouri Supreme Court decision that allows brokers to use standardized forms in a real estate transaction.

147. D. The license law was originally designed in Missouri to protect the public.

148. A. An applicant for a real estate license in the state of Missouri must make a written application. There is no apprenticeship requirement. The application must be made within six months of completing prelicense school, and an applicant must be 18 years of age.

149. C. An applicant may continue to apply for a license even while under investigation. The applicant will not be required to put his or her license on inactive status.

150. A. An applicant who is denied a license must be notified by the Missouri Real Estate Commission of the reason for the denial in writing. The applicant may appeal this decision to the administrative hearing commission. The applicant will not file a complaint with HUD, and there is no ten-day requirement.

151. C. When applying on the required written application for salesperson license, the application must have the signatures of the sponsoring broker and the salesperson.

152. A. Any changes in home address of a licensee are due to the commission within ten days.

153. B. The Missouri Real Estate Commission may file for a restraining order against unlicensed persons for performing acts that require a license or against a licensee for performing acts in violation of the license law. The commission may not file criminal charges or fine the person involved.

154. A. The state association of REALTORS® does not select the real estate commission members. The commission makes and enforces rules. The exams are written under the supervision of the commission and administered by an independent testing company. An executive director administers the operations of the commission.

155. C. In this position, the on-site manager is exempt from the licensing requirements.

156. B. An individual who receives compensation for procuring prospective buyers or renters of real estate must hold a real estate license. Property owners who rent, sell, or buy property for themselves are exempt from licensing requirements, as are resident property managers and licensed attorneys at law.

157. A. Property owners who rent, sell, or buy property for themselves are exempt from licensing requirements.

158. D. A candidate applying for a real estate license must successfully complete a course of 60 classroom hours at a school accredited by the Missouri Real Estate Commission. No college degree is required, nor is U.S. citizenship.

159. B. In Missouri, a licensee may take a six-hour commission-approved course on managing agricultural property if taught by a commission-approved CE sponsor.

160. D. In Missouri, each salesperson's license expires September 30 of each even-numbered year.

161. C. Anyone engaging in the real estate business must have a license from the Missouri Real Estate Commission. Property owners who rent, sell, or buy property for themselves are exempt from licensing requirements. Constructing houses does not require a real estate license.

162. A. Land court certificates are no longer accepted. A title search and opinion, certificate of title, or a full abstract may be used.

163. A. A licensee on inactive status must complete the prelicense course within six months prior to reactivating the license but is not required to take the license exam. No continuing education is required when a license is inactive. No delinquent fee is required.

164. A. A licensee on inactive status must complete the prelicense course within six months prior to reactivating the license but is not required to take the license exam.

165. A. A licensee whose license is on inactive status must pay the biennial renewal fee but is not required to complete continuing education or the prelicense course. The licensee may remain on inactive status for an indefinite period of time as long as the biennial renewal fees are paid.

166. D. A person who receives a "work permit" from the Missouri Real Estate Commission may work in the real estate business in the same way as when a license is issued.

167. D. A person who receives a temporary license from the Missouri Real Estate Commission may only close pending transactions and close the business. The temporary license may not be used to solicit buyers or listings.

168. B. In Missouri, a broker who is a franchise member must file the franchise agreement with the state of Missouri.

169. C. The broker must clearly state in advertising that he or she owns and operates the real estate company. The broker is not required to register the franchise with the local Board of REALTORS®. The franchise is not responsible for the broker's actions, and the franchise name may be used in advertising.

170. D. A broker must state that the franchiser is not liable for the broker's actions on listing agreements, contracts, and closing statements, but is liable in advertising.

171. D. A licensee is not a licensed attorney and may not give legal advice. This could result in a violation of the license law. When asked a legal question, the licensee should advise a buyer to consult with an attorney.

172. C. In Missouri, a licensee must have a signed listing agreement to show property. In this instance, the proper arrangements, i.e., listing agreement, must be obtained first before she may show the property to the buyer.

173. C. License fees, whether for a new license or renewing a license, may be paid by personal check, money order, or cashier's check, but not by cash.

174. A. A salesperson may close a transaction, but only with the supervising broker in attendance. The supervising broker is required to sign the closing statement, not the salesperson, listing broker, or listing broker's salesperson.

175. C. The responsibility for delivery of the closing statement to both buyer and seller is always the listing broker's, no matter who closes the transaction.

176. A. A salesperson may close only under the direct supervision of the sponsoring broker. The sponsoring broker is responsible for signing the closing statement.

177. A. The responsibility for delivery of the closing statement to both buyer and seller is always the listing broker's, no matter who closes the transaction. If there are errors, this responsibility falls on the listing broker, who is responsible for review of the closing statement prior to closing.

178. B. A salesperson may close only under the direct supervision of the sponsoring broker. The salesperson's sponsoring broker is responsible for signing the closing statement.

179. C. The lender is responsible for preparing any promissory notes.

180. B. The broker receives the commission check at closing, in this example, June 10.

181. D. Conducting a title search may lead to charges of practicing law without a license. The broker or salesperson may provide net data and time schedule, explain closing procedures, coordinate inspections, and deliver documents and escrow monies to the appropriate attorney.

182. D. All of these legal descriptions are used in Missouri.

183. B. Legal age, with no exceptions, is 18; some exceptions may enable a 16-year-old to sign certain contracts.

184. D. No action may be maintained against the minor at any time, unless the minor has ratified the contract after becoming 18. There are specific actions in the Missouri statutes that constitute ratification.

185. D. Property managers who are doing these activities under the direct instructions of the property owner are exempt from licensure.

186. B. The exact amount of rent for each unit is not required because of the difficulty in making rent changes. A description of the property, manager's compensation, and the exact documents that must be provided by the manager to the owner are required in a property management agreement.

187. B. In Missouri, the provision is unenforceable, but the lease is still valid.

188. D. The landlord should present the rules when the tenant is entering into the rental agreement or whenever the rules are adopted. Waiting until requested or after the tenant violates them is too late.

189. C. The tenant must notify the landlord and supply instructions and passwords.

190. C. The administrative hearing commission must find a licensee guilty before the Missouri Real Estate Commission can administer any penalty, including revocation of the licensee's license. The Missouri Real Estate Commission does not send all complaints to the administrative hearing commission, only those where it suspects a violation. The administrative hearing commission may make penalty recommendations, but the Missouri Real Estate Commission sets the penalty.

191. C. When a licensee is suspected of a violation, the complaint is sent to the AHC for a hearing. The administrative hearing commission will determine guilt or innocence, and if the licensee is found guilty, the AHC may or may not make recommendations for penalty to the Missouri Real Estate Commission. The Missouri Real Estate Commission sets the penalty. The administrative hearing commission may not take control of a real estate business, investigate a complaint, or impose a penalty.

192. C. Appeals concerning revocation of a licensee's license are made to the circuit court.

193. B. If an applicant is refused a license, the applicant may appeal this decision from the Missouri Real Estate Commission to the administrative hearing commission.

194. A. While recording a deed is not required for the deed to be valid between the grantor and the grantee, or as to persons with actual knowledge of the deed, deeds should be recorded as soon as possible to safeguard the rights of the grantee against claims of third parties.

195. C. The document must be acknowledged. It need not be witnessed by two persons or drawn up by an attorney.

196. A. Taxes become due on December 31 and become a lien on the property on January 1.

197. C. A disabled veteran would have to pay tax on his or her house. Exempt properties include cemeteries, federal government buildings, and private schools.

198. A. Taxes are due on December 31, and become a lien on the property on January 1.

199. A. In Missouri, tenancy by the entireties is extinguished upon the divorce and converts to tenancy in common.

200. D. In Missouri, unless stated to the contrary in a deed, ownership of land by a married couple is assumed to be by tenancy by the entireties.